PUBLISHER'S NOTE:

Among the many things you will soon discover in the pages of this rare and often shocking publication is a hard truth: for an elf, it can be a terribly long fall from respected employee in the world's most famous toy-making workshop to wrangler of human children waiting to see a phony (and often drunk and belligerent) Santa Claus at the mock North Pole display in your neighborhood shopping mall. Such, it seems, was the fate of Snarky, whose copy of the North Pole Employee Handbook you now hold in your hands.

It was Carl Rutherford, an unsuspecting truck driver at a Newark, New Jersey warehouse, who first stumbled upon what looked to him like a conventional employee manual, one not that different from the manual distributed to workers at his own shipping firm; one detailing rules, regulations, and the proper procedures to follow in pursuing a fruitful working relationship with one's employer. If Carl had not been sent to collect discarded Christmas costumes and displays from a recently-closed department store, he may not have even thought much of the name of the company on the front of the handbook: Claus Manufacturing, LLC. The fact that the book had fallen out of a box of elf costumes and seemed to be lightly stained with the amber liquid from a bottle of rye whiskey (also found in the costume box) sent Carl's imagination churning.

When Carl took the North Pole Employee Handbook to his friend Andrew Northram, literature professor at Columbia University, Northram in turn passed it on to Colleen Macintosh, a researcher at the Smithsonian Institution and friend to this publishing house. Handling the pages with a reverence and delicacy normally reserved for the examination of ancient yak vellum, Ms. Macintosh was slowly able to confirm that what you are about to peruse is indeed a copy of the actual employee manual used by Santa's elves.

Snarky, the disgruntled elf whose random and embittered commentary can be found in the margins of this tome, was, as near as our research can uncover, a one-time valued worker in the enterprises of Claus Manufacturing whose increasingly poor attitude and many transgressions led him to be downsized from the North Pole operations. Angry at his dismissal, and perhaps wishing the world could find out about the harsh and often Orwellian conditions at his former workplace, Snarky managed to escape with his procedural manual in hand. Why he then kept it to himself is the great mystery of our involvement in this matter, as is the whereabouts of Snarky himself. He may well be over a hundred years old, and could have borne witness to the many changes in Santa's North Pole operation that have undoubtedly occurred prior to the issuance of this most recent employee manual. But despite our repeated attempts to find out what became of Snarky after he finally hung up his fuzzy hat and left the shopping-mall circuit, no trace of him exists.

Perhaps the power of the great man Santa Claus, and his perceived wrath, was what kept Snarky from blowing the whistle. Perhaps he was just an unrepentant drunk who could never motivate himself to do what he felt in his heart. Whatever the case, and wherever he is now, he did not come forward to claim authorship of, nor indeed any controlling interest in the release of, this publication. Our legal department assures us we have shown due diligence, and that he would not have a leg to stand on at this point.

Therefore we publish *The North Pole Employee Handbook* in his honor, and to offer our readers a glimpse into the everyday workings of a faraway location deeply engrained in our childhood subconscious. There, in a long-thought-enchanted land, exists a company we might at first assume to be very unlike the workplaces in which the rest of us toil each day. Whether it is or not is for you to decide, but this historic discovery—the volume you now hold in your hands—asks us to, at the very least, re-examine the place a certain jolly fat man has held in our heart of hearts. Could we have known, before these ensuing pages brought them to light, about Santa's animosity toward Rudolph, and the ongoing power struggle between the two? Of the chortling fat man who weeps quietly to himself about a traumatic childhood? Of a North Pole workshop so consumed with the bottom line that elves have little to none of the pull we thought they had? Nothing, you will soon discover, is as it seems.

Lastly, it should be noted that we tried to reach a representative of Claus Manufacturing, LLC, but the North Pole and its workshop headquarters are sealed off to all attempts at third-party communication.

To Snarky, wherever he is, we affectionately dedicate this book. And pointedly remind him that he has no legal recourse.

John F. Whalen, Jr.
Cider Mill Press

THE
NORTH POLE
EMPLOYEE
HANDBOOK

THE NORTH POLE EMPLOYEE HANDBOOK

13-Digit ISBN: 978-1-60433-043-4
10-Digit ISBN: 1-60433-043-0

This book may be ordered by mail from the publisher.
Please include $2.50 for postage and handling.
Please support your local bookseller first!

Books published by Cider Mill Press Book Publishers are available at special discounts for bulk purchases in the United States by corporations, institutions, and other organizations. For more information, please contact the publisher.

Cider Mill Press Book Publishers
"Where good books are ready for press"
12 Port Farm Road
Kennebunkport, Maine 04046

Visit us on the web!
www.cidermillpress.com

Cover Design by: Bashan Aquart, Claus Manufacturing, LLC Design Team
Interior Design by: Alicia Freile, Designer Elf Extraordinaire
Illustrations by: Kath Mayer, Illustrator Elf, North Pole Industries
Typography: Galliard, Olduvai, and Christmas Ornaments

Images Copyright © 2008: Robert Adrian Hillman, Darryl Sleath, Charles Taylor, Najib, Najin
All used under license from Shutterstock.com

Printed in China

1 2 3 4 5 6 7 8 9 0
First Edition

– TABLE OF CONTENTS –

Section	Page

1. A WELCOME FROM S. CLAUS, CHAIRMAN AND CEO

Let me begin by saying that I have a certain reputation for making a list, checking it twice, then rather brazenly deciding who qualifies as naughty and who rates as nice. Be assured that this behavioral standard is applied only to the greedy, largely undeserving rabble we in the toy distribution business call "end users," and not to the valued staff of our North Pole gift manufacturing headquarters. And that, my friend, means you! *Blowhard!*

Notice e left out "paid." I want the North Pole to be a place where you, the employee, feel supported and encouraged. That being said, it is probably worth mentioning that you'd better watch out, you'd better not cry, and you'd better not pout. You are a representative of one of the oldest, most established myths in history, and, as such, you will be working sometimes round the clock to manufacture an array of whimsical products. Nothing puts the kibosh on whimsy like a Gloomy Gus or Glenda who finds it somehow beneath him or her to put himself or herself at risk of repetitive-motion injuries in order to bring joy to countless innocent yet thankfully (for our business) already materialistic children. Keep in mind, too, that although I ask team members for a certain amount of personal sacrifice, I'm the guy who has to deliver approximately 4,357,281,901 toys, on a non-engine-driven sleigh, to the entire damn world in less than 24 hours. I hope that puts your carpal tunnel syndrome in perspective.

In the past, new hires have inquired about my ability to see you when you're sleeping. Long-pending legal issues (with former employees whom I'm sure you have seen begging on the streets) prevent me from commenting directly on this. As to knowing when you're awake, there is nothing supernatural involved; it can easily be established with a simple phone call. Also, I do not have an overarching sense of whether or not you've been bad or good, but it can't hurt, as a general rule, to be good for goodness' sake.

Our organization has seen many changes since its humble beginnings in Finland nearly a thousand years ago. Though we still tower above the competition in gift-dispensing mythological-figure market share, the increasing demands of technology and a global economy have necessitated adaptability and flexibility. And so it was that the early-1980s buyout of Claus Manufacturing, LLC, by our parent company Bowl Full of Jelly, Inc., has helped us to grow and remain competitive. By enfolding a variety of other icons under its corporate umbrella (The Easter Bunny, Cupid, and St. Patrick, to name a few), BFJ has established a brand unlike any other.

Rest assured, we remain an independent entity here at Claus Manufacturing, LLC. I won't bore you with the latest research on our demographics and public perception of our corporate identity, but suffice to say you are upholding the jolly, caring, and seemingly philanthropic image of one of the most recognizable symbols in the known universe. Whatever they told you about the importance of your presentation back when you were a barista at Starbucks, multiply that by about a trillion.

It is a privilege and a pleasure, despite the increasing lack of chimneys in the world, to do what I do, and I could not bring joy to the girls and boys without the concerted efforts of you, my North Pole employees. This handbook should answer any questions you may have about proper procedure and conduct.

One final note: I have a stereotype to uphold as a jolly fat man, and therefore am not overly sensitive to comments about my weight. Mrs. Claus, on the other hand, would prefer it if you describe her as "pleasingly plump."

slave

We think you will find this a fun, challenging and exciting place to ~~work~~. On behalf of Mrs. Claus and myself, welcome to the *dysfunctional* family!

—Santa

2. DISCLAIMER

his handbook should be used as a reference guide for providing yourself with key information regarding employment at Claus Manufacturing, LLC. It does not imply a legal contract of any kind, nor should it be used as a substitute for open communication with your immediate supervisor. It is merely a tool.

Aren't we all!

3. EQUAL EMPLOYMENT OPPORTUNITY STATEMENT

I t is the policy of Claus Manufacturing, LLC, not to discriminate on the basis of non-elfdom. It is a fact that the majority of our workers are Elfin-Americans. They are nimble and quick (important factors in our ongoing efficiency) and speak in high-pitched voices (which makes complaints seem far less serious—and even humorous—thus providing a time-honored way to undercut disagreements with a dismissive chuckle). However, we will not refuse work to any qualified candidate who can exhibit the above-mentioned qualifications, be they human, troll, or yeti. *Elvish has left the building.*

Similarly, we will not discriminate based on sex, race, color, ethnic origin, age, religion, disability, sexual orientation, or gender identity. As to the latter, we assume that if you are willing to pull on a pair of striped tights and wear a waistcoat cinched with a wide leather belt, you are at the very least open-minded.

4. HARASSMENT POLICY

The following behaviors constitute harassment:

a. Flicking of stocking-cap pom-pom
b. Inappropriate use of the phrase "jingle bells"
c. Unwanted straightening of curly-toe booties
d. Recitation of limericks that begin with the phrase "There once was an elf from Nantucket … "
e. Whistling, other than while you work
f. Suggestive comments involving the words "sleigh ride"

These behaviors will not be tolerated and will result in immediate review and potential dismissal. Especially behavior d.

5. ORIENTATION PERIOD

All new employees are required to participate in the Claus Manufacturing, LLC, Orientation Program. Devised and developed by our parent company, Bowl Full of Jelly, Inc., the program consists of attendance at *Big Brother* various off-site seminars and team-building exercises designed to ~~introduce~~ *indoctrinate* you to a ~~goal-oriented~~ mindset in which all employees can ~~thrive~~. *allow resentments to fester like an open wound*

Orientation programs include, but are not limited to, such events as:

❄ **Walking on Cold Coals** — Anyone can walk across hot coals, but few can step barefoot across these coldest-of-cold coals, chilled by the Arctic blasts of a North Pole winter. Unleash the iciness lurking in your heart and tap into the ruthlessness you need to succeed in business! Every participant is given a souvenir coal to put into someone's stocking.

※ **Who Croaked Santa?** — This is an interactive murder mystery created in collaboration with top psychologists, the theory being that if all new employees can playfully imagine their boss having been murdered, any unhealthy impulses will be channeled through humorous role-playing and expunged before the employee enters the workforce. *Yeah. That worked REAL well.*

The scenario: Saint Nick, fat as ever, lies dead on the floor in a pool of blood. *Would that it were true*

Whodunit? Was it Frosty? Rudolph? The Grinch? Or you? Playfully sick fun for everyone!

※ **Poetry Workshop** — By encouraging each employee to explore his or her "inner poet," this workshop asks each of us to unlock inner creativity and apply new modes of thinking to problem-solving in the workplace. What beautiful poetry is waiting to come out of *you*?

*Roses Are Red
Violets are Blue
Santa's A suckbag
And I am too (for working here)*

❄ **Keynote Inspirational Speaker: The Dalai Lama** — The great spiritual leader presents the topic *How You Are Actually Contributing to World Peace By Toiling at the North Pole for Minimum Wage With Little or No Benefits.*

6. JOB DESCRIPTIONS AND DUTIES

t other companies, the phrase "cog in the wheel" has a negative connotation. Not here at the North Pole! In fact, we looked up "cog" in the dictionary, and guess what we found? Here's what it means:

One of a series of teeth on the rim of a wheel which, when engaged, transmits motive force to the operation of the wheel itself

That's right, North Pole Cog, you are *transmitting motive force* with each and every task you perform! *Now* do you feel like you're part of something? You bet you do. Are you some boring old "associate" or "team member"? No! You're a cog! And all we ask is that you be one of the happiest, most complaint-free cogs the world has ever known.

Each North Pole Cog has a specific function to perform. Those functions are as follows:

A. Entry-Level Cogs

Balsa-Wood Shavings Maintenance — Responsible for the immediate collection and disposal of all balsa-wood shavings associated with the making of wooden race-cars, trains, puzzles, building blocks, and alphabet blocks. Other duties include, but are not limited to, pick-up of discarded and/or defective plastic dinosaur appendages; removal of broken beaker shards from "My First Chemistry Set" output; and giving backrubs to senior toymakers.

Reindeer Droppings Engineer — Your supervisor will go over the details of this position with you. Suffice to say we convert the waste produced by Rudolph and company into fuel (one of the many side ventures of Bowl Full of Jelly, Inc., that ensures our continued profitability), and someone has to shove it all into the machine that grinds it up and spits it out. (The thing is, it's often clogged, and you really have to get in there and push. Anyway, again, discuss this with your immediate supervisor.) ANTIBIOTICS AVAILABLE UPON REQUEST.

Pharmaceuticals!

Gift Sacker — Responsible for the insertion of all prepped gifts into one of Santa's many canvas sacks for sleigh delivery. NOTE: The Gift Sacker reports to the Gift Wrapper (see "Middle-Management Positions," below). Under no circumstances should the Gift Sacker interfere with the Gift Wrapper, nor should the Gift Wrapper put undue pressure on the Gift Sacker to the point where the Gift Sacker cannot match the output of the Gift Wrapper such that it leads to the Gift Sacker causing damage to the Gift Wrapper's output, thereby necessitating the repetition of the process by which the Gift Wrapper completes the Gift wrapping and gives it to the Gift Sacker, who does the Gift sacking. It is a given that the above is self-explanatory.

Bow-Finger Technician — The B-FT holds his or her index finger down on the ribbon while the Gift Wrapper ties off each delightful bow on each beautifully wrapped package.

B. Assembly Line Cogs

Foundation Shape Creation Specialist — Responsible for inserting initial unformed block of wood or plastic into our patented ShapeSpewer™ device. Hands off resulting foundation items (race car, caboose, building block, baby head and torso, velociraptor, etc.) to Supplemental Attachment Engineer for completion.

Supplemental Attachment Engineer — The all-important wheels are your responsibility, as are legs, arms, and talons. NOTE: Your supervisor is instructed to issue severe reprimands for such actions as going "vroom-vroom" with your completed race car. As tempting as it is to sample the life-affirming nature of our product, remember this simple company motto if you want to last at the North Pole:

THERE IS NO SUCH THING AS AN INNER CHILD

You will find this motto posted at several locations convenient to your workstation. We suggest you glance up at it as often as possible. *glance up at this!*

Teddy Bear and Baby Eye Sticker-Onner — It is this cog's responsibility to glue black onyx eyes onto all plush toys created by the Stuffed Animal Workshop (see "Middle Management"), and onto the baby heads generated by the Foundation Shape Creation Specialist. Any complaints regarding anxiety caused by staring at lifeless eyes all day should be directed immediately to Mrs. Claus in Human Resources.

Toy Assembly Shift Supervisor — Responsible for overseeing all assembly line production of wooden and plastic toys. You must maintain particular vigilance while monitoring the production of the Red Ryder Carbine-Action Range Model Air Rifle with the compass in the stock and the thing that tells time. Simply put, we do not want anyone putting an eye out.

Electronic and Hand-Held Play Device Assembly — This position is currently outsourced to Beijing. *Tell me about it!*

C. Specialty Cogs

Stocking Stuffers — As world population has increased, it has become impossible for Santa to take the time to individually stuff stockings. Between the roof-landing, chimney-entering (where applicable), cookies-and-milk consumption, and presents-under-the-tree distribution, your CEO is seriously resource-constrained. Therefore, the SS is responsible for maintaining a steady inventory of chocolate drops, miniature books containing inspiring quotations, candy canes, key chains, iPods (when consistent with recipient's level of income), oranges (U.K. only), pens that depict a woman undressing when you tip them upside down (when consistent with recipient's level of education), and other whimsical items. The efficient stocking stuffer should have up to six recipients' stockings filled with Crapola™ (our own line of North Pole mini-gifts) in the time it takes Santa to wolf down a couple of hardened sugar cookies, suck down some low-fat milk to keep him from gagging on them, and fling the recipients' gifts under the tree.

Let the fat man choke!

As a specialty Stocking-Stuffer cog, your training consists of real-time stuffing of half a dozen average-sized stockings hung from a replica mantelpiece. Simulated on-site variables will also be included, such as stockings that are poorly push-pinned to the mantel (these will drop when fully loaded and must be re-tacked), or hard-to-read names on the stockings themselves, which can result in non-sex-appropriate placement of gifts (chances are "Joe" is not going to know how to react to the tiger-print thong).

NOTE: A recently added position at Claus Manufacturing, LLC, the SS is the first cog in history to travel along with Santa on his rounds. No one has ever before been privy to the experience of flying through the air on a reindeer-driven sleigh.

Therefore, anonymity is essential. As is packing those pills that prevent you from throwing up. *Not to mention sitting next to the fat old GAS-BAG and behind 1,600 pounds of fur-covered venison!*

Online Ordering Virus Creators — This is another recently added position at Claus Manufacturing, LLC, one that is absolutely fundamental to the continued success of our North Pole operations. Basically, someone has to stop people from ordering their Christmas gifts online.

Claus Manufacturing, LLC, leads the world in the recruitment of young, elfin Internet geniuses, and we are way out in front when it comes to using these gifted elves to make sure we retain our demographic supremacy. Last year alone, an exceedingly clever little bug advised 50 million online-ordering clients of six major retailers that over 10,000 different items were "no longer in stock."

Rest assured, we continue to improve our sabotaging of technology in an effort to maintain the viability of you, our work force.

D. Site Maintenance Cogs

Sleigh Detailer — Santa is extremely particular about his sleigh. You may feel that there is no reason to fully detail a sleigh every day when it will only be used for one evening out of the year. You must resist the urge to say, let alone think, this. The waxing, polishing and vacuuming of "Norman" (that's what Santa calls the sleigh ... we've never been able to figure out why) is a duty not to be taken lightly.

Reindeer Stable Hand — Responsible for feeding, brushing, and exercising Donder *et al.* The low rate of compensation for this position is more than offset by the opportunities for flying.

Building Maintenance Technician — Tasks include supervision of heating ducts, Christmas lights, and plumbing, and making sure that happy tunes are darn well playing 24/7 on the piped-in Muzak. *make it stop, for the love of God,* MAKE IT STOP!

North Pole Security Officer — This cog checks employee identification at main entrance, maintains order during factory tours, removes graffiti from building exterior, and tells desperate female groupies camped outside the premises to move along.

Freakin' guy gets more action than a businessman in Bangkok. LIFE ISN'T FAIR!!!!

E. Middle-Management Cogs

Stuffed Animal Workshop Denizen — Three years' apprenticeship is required for this demanding position. We at Claus Manufacturing, LLC, are justifiably proud of our hand-sewn teddy bears, bunny rabbits, and other plush animals. We typically promote up to 20 entry-level cogs into the coveted SAWD slots each winter. NOTE: Denizens caught sleeping with their plush toys are subject to immediate dismissal. Those found carrying on imaginary conversations in baby voice with their plush toys (e.g., "Who's a good boy?") will be put on notice. Your supervisor is instructed to discourage you from clutching, squeezing, or otherwise forming an attachment to your stuffed animal in any way. Several of the aforementioned "There is no such thing as an inner child" warnings are posted in plain view throughout the Stuffed Animal Workshop.

Gift Wrapper — Primary duties include wrapping presents for girls and boys, tying off ribbons/bows (in conjunction with the Bow Finger Technician, see above), and making sure packages are not scuffed, scraped, or torn in transit. In this task, the Gift Wrapper is greatly aided by the Gift Sacker (see above), since both the Gift Sacker and the Gift Wrapper can be penalized for damages, whether said damages were caused by the Gift Sacker or the Gift Wrapper. The Gift Wrapper and the Gift Sacker must work in concert to ensure that neither Gift Sacker nor Gift Wrapper exceed a limit of two imperfect packages per day. The Gift Wrapper shall be considered the immediate supervisor to the Gift Sacker, such that the Gift Wrapper bears a greater responsibility than the Gift Sacker for the final product quality at the point at which the Gift Wrapper hands off the completed package to the Gift Sacker. It is a given that the above is self-explanatory.

Office Manager — The primary responsibilities of the OM are replacing the toner in the copy machine and policing the break-room refrigerator for moldy food.

F. Upper Management Cogs:

Director of Myth Maintenance — This is one of the most closely guarded positions at the North Pole, and one of the biggest reasons for compliance with the nondisclosure agreement. With every passing year, as children grow up faster and become less and less impressionable, they become more resistant to the suspension of disbelief. The position of DMM was created to ensure that Santa and his magical

fascist!

abilities are valued by succeeding generations of families well into the future. It involves everything from making sure retail outlets get their Christmas displays up by Halloween to reporting any department-store Santa whose breath smells like rotgut.

Director of Roof Accessibility — Using Google Earth® technology in conjunction with an extensive network of freelance photographers, the DRA conducts yearly checks on the conditions of roofs around the world and makes sure that any roof that has fallen into disrepair (and is thus incapable of supporting Santa and the reindeer) is declared unfit for that year's list of deliveries.

Director of Alternate Entry — Once a home has been taken off the year's delivery list owing to improper roof maintenance, the DAE, using an extensive network of on-the-ground cat burglars, discovers and identifies possible window/basement/bulkhead entries that Santa may utilize on his Christmas Eve rounds. Other duties include maintaining an up-to-date contact list of suppliers of glass-cutters and suction cups in all areas of the known world. It is not his favorite thing to do, but Santa will break and enter if he has to.

Director of Bogus UFO Phenomena — In order for Santa to make use of the DAE's choices, he must often land in more conspicuous areas. The DBUFOP rapidly generates rumors of nearby crop-circle formations, cattle mutilations, and alien abductions, thereby distracting the general public from the presence of a reindeer-driven sleigh in their vicinity.

We hope this overview of our staff positions and associated duties has helped you to understand the importance of your role to the overall operation of Claus Manufacturing, LLC. Having a working knowledge of the responsibilities of your colleagues can only further your respect for them, and galvanize your ability to be an effective and valued employee. *Actually, it ha galvanized m. determination to drink myself to death.*

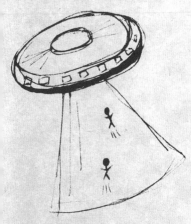

7. THE FIVE CORE COMPETENCIES

The values and corporate vision of Claus Manufacturing, LLC, are reflected in the Five Core Competencies. It is expected that these skills will be utilized each and every North Pole workday. The competencies are as follows:

❄ **Joy** — You are working long and punishing hours, jammed into a crowded workplace with your fellow employees, under pressure to keep up with a worldwide demand for toys, and are often acutely aware of the musty odor of a nearby reindeer stable. Being happy is essential. *up yours!*

❄ *A Cappella* — At any time, and without advance notice, cogs of any rank may be expected to join their co-workers in singing a happy work song. (For songbook, see "Supplemental Materials," Exhibit VI.) The cadence of these impromptu little numbers immediately creates the kind of militaristic precision that can really motivate a workforce.

Your voice raised in song goes a long way in increasing cama-
raderie, speeding up production, and giving us new material
for our promotional sizzle reel.

Who's kidding who? Shoot me now, and end my miserable elf existence!

❄ **Caring About Quality** — (Pride) in what you are helping
to produce here at Claus Manufacturing, LLC, can't help but
translate into maximum enjoyment for the end user. After all,
would *you* want to get a teddy bear with one eye dangling
out of its socket?

❄ **"Pitch-Infulness"** — Is a fellow assembly-line cog
temporarily blinded by a balsa-wood-shard projectile? Are a
Gift Wrapper's paper cuts leaving bloodstains on the packages?
Does Santa have a sudden craving for a meatball sub? Cogs
who step up to help with these and other situations are letting
us know they're the "pitch-innyest"!

❄ **Striving to Improve** — Your success as a cog in this
organization depends on your willingness to better yourself.
We guarantee such self-determination will probably not go
unnoticed for more than a few years.

We hope you will return to the Core Competencies page of this handbook frequently to inspire and motivate yourself. If, however, you are pressed for time, the core competencies *(Joy, A Cappella, Caring About Quality, Pitch-Infulness and Striving to Improve)* can be recalled using this easy-to-remember acronym:

JACCAQPISTI

8. PROBATIONARY PERIOD

There is a 30-day probationary period during which all new hires are evaluated for their performance and compatibility with management and co-workers. Employees terminated within the 30-day probationary period may not contest their fate through the normal grievance procedure (see section 9, below). All further legal definitions of these proceedings may be found in the North Pole City Hall Public Records Office, under the heading "S.O.L."

Evaluations during the probationary period will take into account such topics as:

a. Willingness to take orders and like it. *Like I have a choice!*
b. Proper attitude: demerits for use of inappropriate references such as "Fat Boy," "Rudolph the Brown-Nosed Reindeer,"

or "Merry Friggin' Christmas."

c. Cleanliness & hygiene: infractions involving stubble, halitosis, and excessive hat-head.

d. Concentration & focus: are you fully present in your work, or are visions of sugar plums dancing in your head?

In the back portion of this handbook, you will find a sample evaluation sheet (see "Supplementary Materials, Exhibit II"). Please review this form and become familiar with it so that you may be prepared when we come at you.

9. GRIEVANCES

hould a Claus Manufacturing , LLC, cog feel that he or she has been disciplined in error, that cog should fill out a grievance form. *and prepa for letha injection.* The sample form included at the back of this handbook will guide you step-by-step through the proper way to file your complaint (see "Supplemental Materials," Exhibit III).

~~If this system had actually worked,~~
~~I wouldn't be where I am now.~~

10. IDENTIFICATION CARDS

Make sure to drop by and see Mrs. Claus at the Department of Human Resources for the issuing of your official Claus Manufacturing, LLC, ID card! Having an up-to-date ID will help you enter the premises safely and securely each day—after all, it can be challenging for our Security Officer to tell one set of pointy ears and striped beanie from another!

By accepting your Claus Manufacturing, LLC, ID, you authorize Claus Manufacturing, LLC, to collect and keep on file personal data including, but not limited to, your photograph, address, phone number(s), place of birth, identification numbers (government-issued and otherwise), mother's maiden name, next of kin's name, credit history, school record, vaccination record, psychological evaluation, fingerprints, footprints, and dental chart.

NOTE: The above-mentioned data will never be shared with anyone except recognized and authorized representatives of Claus Manufacturing, LLC; parent company Bowl Full of Jelly, Inc.; corporate counsel Snowman, Snowman, Snowman and Klein; North Pole Savings & Loan; any other bank; any other law firm; the North Pole Department of Corrections; the North Pole Department of Homeland Security; or any other governmental agency (of any government). Absolutely no one else will have access to employee data unless they pay a fee.

11. CONFIDENTIALITY AGREEMENT

 ll new cogs are required to sign and date the confidentiality agreement (see Supplemental Materials, Exhibit I, in the back of this handbook). The day-to-day operations at Claus Manufacturing, LLC, are closely guarded trade secrets, and must never fall into the wrong hands.

Should you find yourself in the wrong hands, biting down on the capsule hidden in the heel of your company-issue curly-toed shoes will prevent any dissemination of confidential information about the inner workings of Claus Manufacturing, LLC. *Shoulda done it when I had the chance.*

12. NON-COMPETE/ EXCLUSIVITY

By agreeing to become a member cog at Claus Manufacturing, LLC, you are consenting to the following:

I. That you shall be employed exclusively by Claus Manufacturing, LLC, and shall not solicit or accept any other offers of work for a period of three years after the date of your hiring.

II. That you shall make yourself available for all regular work hours during the peak holiday manufacturing season (Oct. 15–Jan. 6) for the above-mentioned three-year period.

III. That the three-year non-compete agreement shall include refusal to take on any outside work during designated holiday periods (SEE FOLLOWING SECTION).

13. DESIGNATED HOLIDAY PERIODS

The following are **unpaid** holidays for all Claus Manufacturing, LLC, cogs:

January 7, 8, 9, 10, 11, 12, 13, 14, 15, 16, 17, 18, 19, 20, 21, 22, 23, 24, 25, 26, 27, 28, 29, 30, 31.

February 1, 2, 3, 4, 5, 6, 7, 8, 9, 10, 11, 12, 13, 14, 15, 16, 17, 18, 19, 20, 21, 22, 23, 24, 25, 26, 27, 28/29.

March 1, 2, 3, 4, 5, 6, 7, 8, 9, 10, 11, 12, 13, 14, 15, 16, 17, 18, 19, 20, 21, 22, 23, 24, 25, 26, 27, 28, 29, 30, 31.

April 1, 2, 3, 4, 5, 6, 7, 8, 9, 10, 11, 12, 13, 14, 15, 16, 17, 18, 19, 20, 21, 22, 23, 24, 25, 26, 27, 28, 29, 30.

May 1, 2, 3, 4, 5, 6, 7, 8, 9, 10, 11, 12, 13, 14, 15, 16, 17, 18, 19, 20, 21, 22, 23, 24, 25, 26, 27, 28, 29, 30, 31.

June 1, 2, 3, 4, 5, 6, 7, 8, 9, 10, 11, 12, 13, 14, 15, 16, 17, 18, 19, 20, 21, 22, 23, 24, 25, 26, 27, 28, 29, 30.

July 1, 2, 3, 4, 5, 6, 7, 8, 9, 10, 11, 12, 13, 14, 15, 16, 17, 18, 19, 20, 21, 22, 23, 24, 25, 26, 27, 28, 29, 30, 31.

August 1, 2, 3, 4, 5, 6, 7, 8, 9, 10, 11, 12, 13, 14, 15, 16, 17, 18, 19, 20, 21, 22, 23, 24, 25, 26, 27, 28, 29, 30, 31.

September, 1, 2, 3, 4, 5, 6, 7, 8, 9, 10, 11, 12, 13, 14, 15, 16, 17, 18, 19, 20, 21, 22, 23, 24, 25, 26, 27, 28, 29, 30.

October 1, 2, 3, 4, 5, 6, 7, 8, 9, 10, 11, 12, 13, 14.

During these designated holiday periods, you are encouraged to continue your residency in Claus Manufacturing, LLC, dwellings (see "Housing," Section 19) and take in all the excitement the North Pole has to offer! *like freezing your bells off!*

14. DRESS CODE

Remember that as a cog at Claus Manufacturing, LLC, you represent thousands of years of heartfelt tradition. We ask that you wear the uniform you are issued with pride. The wearing of tights, vest, curly-toed shoes, and a stocking cap with a puffy white fuzzball on the end is like saying "We don't need no stinking badges!" to anyone who questions your importance in the vision of our company. *Humans coming in here and taking our jobs . . they ought to build a wall to keep them outta the Pole*

A NOTE TO OUR HUMAN EMPLOYEES: Please be advised that we do require you to wear fake elf ears whenever you are on the premises. We are more than happy to welcome our human friends to the workshop, but you must have an understanding that you are entering an elf-heavy environment. Insisting that you don plastic ears is not our way of humiliating you (though you are welcome to interpret it that way), but a gesture of solidarity with your fellow employees.

Where was the solidarity when I needed it?

15. DENTAL PLAN

We are proud to offer reduced-rate dental care to all Claus Manufacturing, LLC, cogs through Herbie, a former elf who always wanted to be a dentist. Simply show your Claus Manufacturing, LLC, ID card at time of payment, and receive 30% off all services (crowns not included).

The only one with the stones to do what he really wanted!

Herbie rules!

16. OTHER BENEFITS

N/A

17. POLICY ON CONTROLLED SUBSTANCES

Claus Manufacturing, LLC, has a zero-tolerance policy when it comes to the use of any illegal controlled substances. As to legal, non-controlled substances, in each new hire's locker can be found our welcome gift to you: a complimentary fifth of 180 proof Old Crow. We know the kind of pressure you will be under to produce for the holiday season, and our goal is to make your North Pole experience a happy and painless one. Our welcome gift to you will go a long way toward fulfilling that goal!

18. A NOTE ON THE CONSTANT DARKNESS

One way to look at life during a North Pole winter is that the axial tilt of the earth in relation to its plane of revolution around the sun dictates that we face away from that sun for the winter. Another way to look at it is that outside our building there are 24 hours of total darkness each and every day during peak production times. We hope the welcome gift found in your locker (see above) will help you through the difficult times.

19. HOUSING

By signing our non-compete clause (no pun intended), each cog agrees to be employed exclusively by us for a period of three years. In return for that loyalty, we provide clean and efficient housing so that you do not have to worry about ever leaving the premises. This of course is of significant value to the cog who has been making toys from 5 a.m. to midnight—our most popular "double"—and needs some shut-eye before starting that same shift again a few hours later.

Company housing can also be a boon during the 281 days in which you remain *are kept* here at the North Pole, unable under contract to seek work at any other establishment for, as we said, three years.

One of the unique perks of working here at Claus Manufacturing, LLC, is that we provide free ~~housing~~ *prison* for over two-thirds of the year—it's our good-faith way of saying,

"Come back and see us again next toy season!" *by which time the hollowed-out husk you once called a soul will be ours.*

Keep in mind, too, that the summer months feature 24 hours of daylight each and every day, so you will have your path well-lighted as you explore the many *two* things there are to do on the coldest place on earth!

Our employee housing consists of charming individual cottages that are part of a state-of-the-art complex with a common courtyard and skating rink. We encourage our elves (and humans dressed as elves) to go skating at any time during their five hours off per day. It's great exercise, and adds to the jolly, bucolic atmosphere we strive to cultivate here at Claus Manufacturing, LLC, for when there are cameras present.

Each delightful one-bedroom unit features full kitchen and bath, as well as individual, well-kept, comfortable beds for you and the nine other cogs with whom you will share lodgings.

NOTE: A single laundry room serves the entire cottage complex. This requires cooperation among the ~~tenants~~ *inmates,* and each cog is responsible for budgeting his or her own time for laundry. UNDER NO CIRCUMSTANCES are you to use Mrs. Claus's private top-loader!

20. BREAK TIME

ach and every Claus Manufacturing, LLC, cog is required by law* to receive a five-minute break for every 11-hour shift worked, as well as an 11.5-minute break for lunch. (IMPORTANT: If a cog should neglect to take his or her five-minute break before lunch, the five unused minutes *may not* be added to the lunch break! Our facility must meet an output unheard of in other industries, and we cannot tolerate the drop in productivity that would result from a 16.5-minute lunch.)

 (*Since five different countries lay claim to the North Pole's resources, you can imagine that Claus Manufacturing, LLC, labor disputes involve a mountain of red tape, as well as years of costly legal fees and then, because of jurisdiction issues, usually come to nothing. Just something to think about.)

21. YOUR BREAK ROOM

ow you spend your free time during your generous breaks is up to you, but our break room provides a variety of conveniences of which many cogs may want to avail themselves. They include:

a. A table — Very useful as a surface on which to place things.

b. Chairs — Since a goodly percentage of your job responsibilities involve standing for long periods of time, the three break-room folding chairs are much-sought-after commodities. They may also be used in conjunction with the table.

c. Microwave oven — Works. You may need to consult with IT regarding how to turn it on.

d. Refrigerator — For those cogs who choose not to contribute to the welfare of our organization by taking lunch in our reasonably priced cafeteria (see section 32), a small refrigerator is provided in which sack lunches or food containers may be stored.

Note to self: make sure to store venison in company freezer!

A Few Considerations Regarding the Refrigerator

✻ Please keep the temperature setting on high, as the fridge tends to underperform and not keep things very cold.

✻ In fact, some employees have found that simply leaving their food in a snow bank during their shift can be more effective for storing perishables.

✻ When taking advantage of the aforementioned snow bank, be advised that your foodstuffs will often become frozen solid, and could present difficulties should they need to be consumed within your allotted 5- and 11.5-minute breaks.

✻ Obviously, if you bring an item that can be thawed in a microwave, then you could most likely get it eaten within your scheduled time. Before, we were talking about if you brought a sandwich or salad or fruit or something. Those are the things that could be difficult to deal with when frozen.

❄ All of this makes a case for using the cafeteria, by the way.

Lastly, be sure to write your name on your lunchbag or food container so that a fellow cog will have no excuse when asked why he or she ate something that wasn't his or hers. All unclaimed food left in the refrigerator for over seven days shall be disposed of. Especially yogurt. For some reason there's always a thing of yogurt sitting there.

e. Suggestion box — In the far left corner of the break room, by the dispenser of waterless hand sanitizer, mounted on the underside of a fiberboard cabinet in which nothing is kept, you will find a small, locked metal box with an opening on its face big enough to fit a folded piece of paper. This is your suggestion box. We at Claus Manufacturing, LLC, welcome any and all feedback from our cogs as to how to improve the atmosphere, working conditions, or efficiency of our operations.

In the Supplemental Materials section (Exhibit IV) you will find a sample Employee Feedback Form. Please make photocopies of this form, available for 75 cents per page at company store Hung By the Chimney (see section 33) whenever you wish to communicate with the corporation as to what makes a cog like you think we can do our jobs better.

Employee feedback can be anonymous; you are not required to identify yourself. But should you have a constructive suggestion, having been informed of the location of the break room suggestion box, you now know where to stick it.

22. INTER-EMPLOYEE DATING

Claus Manufacturing, LLC, maintains a strict anti-intra-establishment dating policy. We acknowledge that this policy may be at odds with the ready availability of mistletoe on the premises, but we cannot stress our viewpoint strongly enough: becoming emotionally involved with another cog is highly detrimental to productivity, as well as being a rather sickening sight to the rest of us. The following are just a few of the ways in which cog-on-cog romance hurts the work environment:*

❋ Everyone knows you're doing it. *Yeah, baby!*
❋ Your disgusting after-hours trysts have you reporting for work fatigued and making mistakes. And on-the-job errors in this field can result in the blindness, dismemberment, or even death of your fellow cogs. Think about that the next time you can't keep it in your tunic.
❋ The workplace romance inevitably runs its course, leaving

each party embittered, vengeful, and far from having the sunny personality required to maintain our consistent quality output. Plus, now everybody knows you're not doing it.

(*Source: Sturmundrang, Dieter. *Concerning Unhealthy Sexual Dynamics in the Adult Elf While Employed At Claus Manufacturing, LLC.* Commissioned by Bowl Full of Jelly, Inc.; published by Big Black Boot Press, an imprint of S. Claus Enterprises. 1956.)

As you can see, a relationship with a fellow employee is something to be avoided at all costs. And should Human Resources become aware of it, the infraction will be severely disciplined, up to and including the imposing of several weeks without pay. Remember that Mrs. Claus, our head of Human Resources, has her own problems with being physically neglected during the peak production times when Santa is rarely available to her. This does not make her sympathetic to your situation. When it comes to an inter-workshop romance, take note of this simple rule of thumb:

Mrs. Claus WILL take you down.

Oh, well, that's $11 you'll never see again.

23. HE SEES YOU WHEN YOU'RE SLEEPING

Owing to pending legal action, this section temporarily omitted.

Previously ~~gro~~ ~~d,~~
fic
~~ne~~
~~'t~~
~~ts~~
~~h~~
~~g~~
~~o~~ ~~s~~
~~q~~
~~cc~~
~~cc~~
~~wi~~
~~th~~
~~thr~~ ... in no uncertain terms

Sees you when you're SLEEPING? What a load of crap! FAT BOY put hidden cameras all over the place, and the Department of Myth Maintenance is suppressing it so everyone will still think he has supernatural powers. FASCIST!

24. SICK LEAVE

Of course we would prefer it if each cog worked all of the scheduled hours assigned to him or her. We realize, however, that certain health concerns *alcohol poison* may prevent an employee from performing at an optimum level, and that in such cases said employee might opt to take a sick day.

Claus Manufacturing, LLC has established several helpful guidelines as to the definition of "sick," which we trust will be of significant value as you contemplate whether or not to shirk your duties. They are as follows:

A cold — This is the North Pole. Having a cold is often a near-constant state of existence. Therefore we do not allow sick days for this condition. Should the symptoms progress from "cold" to "flu" (e.g., with chills, fever, vomiting, diarrhea, etc.), a sick day will be allowed, especially since it would be prudent not to risk giving such a virus to your fellow cogs. We can all agree that the last thing we need is an assembly line full of shaking, sweating, projectile-vomiting, feces-stained elves.

Injury — Without question, the loss of a limb is a serious enough problem to merit at least half a day off. With a more minor injury, such as the loss of a single digit, time off will depend upon how individual productivity is affected. Rest assured that should anything as serious as the former occur, we do have an on-site medical professional. Herbie the Dentist has a full complement of shiny, modern, official-looking machines that resemble the things you might see in a real medical facility.

Personal wellness — The concept of a "personal day" is not tolerated at Claus Manufacturing, LLC. You do not have the luxury of needing to take time for yourself. You have been entrusted with the hopes and dreams of millions of the world's children, many of whom are disadvantaged, hospitalized with terrible diseases, or experiencing a nagging feeling of incompleteness that will not be assuaged until they get an erector set. Your job is to put the well-being of these children first. Your "wellness" is of no concern to them.

25. LETTERS TO SANTA

r. Claus receives over 4 million letters every holiday season, and he cannot possibly answer them all himself. From time to time, every Claus Manufacturing, LLC, cog will be required to perform letter-answering duties on his behalf. The worksheet in the back of this handbook (see "Supplemental Materials," Exhibit V) provides the do's and don'ts you will need to take into consideration when responding to the children of the world.

26. THE TWELVE DAYS OF CHRISTMAS AND WHAT THEY MEAN TO YOU

Various faiths have different ways of commemorating the period from Christmas Day through January 6 (Twelfth Night). Knowing how representatives of these many forms of worship celebrate is not a prerequisite for cogs employed by Claus Manufacturing, LLC. However, since there are Twelve Days of Christmas, this means that our work does not end on the morning of December 25.

Though on a far less punishing schedule, Santa and the reindeer are expected to make a healthy portion of overnight deliveries on other dates during this block of time. Over the years, we have found it cost-effective to subcontract for the items most in demand from 12/25 to 1/6. As such, it is the responsibility of these outside vendors to keep a steady stock of goods ready for Santa, and cogs will need to make regular runs on certain dates to the following suppliers:

❄ Dec. 25 — A PARTRIDGE IN A PEAR TREE. *Birds In Trees 4 U, 2312 Ice Shelf Terrace, Frozen Town.* Ron & Carrie Schlossberg, props.

❄ Dec. 26 — TWO TURTLE DOVES. Same as above.

❄ Dec. 27 — THREE FRENCH HENS. *Crazy Freddie's Climate-Controlled Livestock Emporium, Polar Ice Cap 23, Apt. 9, Cold Springs.* Alex Smythe, prop. (Freddie died some time back.)

❄ Dec. 28 — FOUR CALLING BIRDS. *Birds in Trees 4 U Specialty Annex, 16 Magnetic North Blvd., Chilling.* By appointment only.

❄ Dec. 29 — FIVE GOLDEN RINGS. *Irv's Fine Jewelry and Seal Meat, 36 Ice Floe Plaza, Brrville.* Irv Slop, prop.

❄ Dec. 30 — SIX GEESE A-LAYING. *Melissa's Free-Range, Organically-Fed Geese, 2 Frigid Farm Rd., Witch's Teat.*

Melissa Starchild, owner and oracle. *(Geese kept in constant state of egg production by non-invasive hypnotherapy.)*

❄ Dec. 31 — SEVEN SWANS A-SWIMMING. *Swans 'n More! 6853 Snowpack Terrace, Chatterteeth.* Walt "Got Ya!" Scofield, prop.

❄ Jan. 1 — EIGHT MAIDS A-MILKING. *Frank's Esoteric Requests, Inc., Melting Glacier 9, Quadrant 6B, Greenland-adjacent.* Frank, prop.

❄ Jan. 2 — NINE LADIES DANCING. *Vinnie's Hot Chicks Rental, 38 Ice Floe Plaza, Brrville.* Vinnie Fugettaboutit, prop.

❄ Jan. 3 — TEN LORDS A-LEAPING. *Nigel's Fey British Dandy Service, 809 Frozen Ave., Frigid.* Nigel Mannering-Swithen-Wimple, prop.

❄ Jan. 4 — ELEVEN PIPERS PIPING. *Everything Eleven! 54 Icicle Row, Parka Town.* Franchise owners vary.

❄ Jan. 5— TWELVE DRUMMERS DRUMMING. *One-Stop Out-of-Work Musician Services, 302 Numb Extremities Circle, Shiverton.* Willie "Mad Dog" Sticks, prop.

27. TREE TRIMMING

The Claus Manufacturing, LLC, Christmas tree is the largest Christmas tree in the known universe. *almost as big as Santa's ego!* Previously grown by magical fairies in Santa's native Finland, the Claus holiday tree is now harvested in a secret Pacific Northwest location by the U.S. government, after the Department of Forestry made the fairies an offer they couldn't refuse and used their skills to create the impossibly enormous Tannenbaum under controlled conditions. At 152 feet high and 41 feet in diameter, when this glorious abnormality is lit up three weeks before Christmas it makes the tree at Rockefeller Plaza look like the light bulb in your refrigerator as viewed from outer space.

All cogs must log in at least eight hours work on tree-trimming procedure, which takes a total of seven weeks. The sprightly and agile nature of elves comes in particularly handy for this detail, since budgetary concerns mean there are no ladders, rigging or hydraulic platforms used.

Typically, a small team of around 20 or 30 elves can string one row of tinsel around the tree in just under five days. It is quite a sight to see our holiday tree literally crawling with cogs, each one an integral part of the visual symmetry to come. And if you're worried about being out in the bitter, windy cold, take heart in knowing that Mrs. Claus is right out there with you, standing at the base of the tree and shouting through a bullhorn, letting you know in no uncertain terms exactly what is—and isn't—working for her. *Leona Helmsley in fleece!*

Perhaps the most sought-after position on the tree trimming crew is that of the elf who climbs all the way to the top of our tall, tall tree to put the star on its very top. (NOTE: At orientation everyone should have been given the handout containing information about the North Pole's own reasonably priced personal injury law firm.)

28. PROPER CONDUCT AROUND THE REINDEER

Santa's nine reindeer friends are a vital component in the delivery of our product to the end users. UNDER NO CIRCUMSTANCES SHOULD YOU FEED OR PET THE REINDEER. We understand that they are visually striking creatures. We realize that the proximity of their holding pen to a common employee area (i.e., the break room) is a problem. Rest assured that we are working to find a solution, and have been since the year 1352.

In the meantime, keep in mind that reindeer are high-strung by nature. They have all been spayed and/or neutered, and they live forever. With that in mind, the best policy when it comes to the reindeer is to avoid eye contact. It freaks them out.

There are some employees involved in the Christmas Eve delivery preparations, such as the Stable Hand and Reindeer Droppings Engineer (see "Job Descriptions and Duties," section 6), who must by necessity interact with the reindeer. For these employees, we offer a breakdown of the distinct personality traits of each animal, in order that behavior may be adjusted around them accordingly:

❄ DASHER — Came by her name rightly. Will bolt as if beginning deliveries at the slightest hint of a sack of toys nearby. Can smell wrapping paper at 50 yards. (NOTE: Any Dasher-related accidents are not covered under our Health Plan.)

❄ DANCER — Fairly docile until he hears disco music. (See "Banned Music," Elf Socials, Section 31, part b.)

❄ PRANCER — Same as above, but more prone to sudden outbursts. At all costs, avoid playing Village People recordings around this reindeer.

❄ VIXEN — Extremely oversexed. Once tried to mate with a divan.

Nice rack!

✳ COMET — Usually the reindeer no one remembers. As far as we know, hasn't done anything wrong.

Real name is Stupid! ✳ CUPID — Insufferable *yenta*. Has been trying to hook up Dasher and Donder for years, despite strict company policies on inter-workhorse relations.

✳ DONDER —Laid-back to a fault, very hard to motivate. A surfer dude with fur. DO NOT honor his so-called prescription for medical marijuana.

✳ BLITZEN — Party animal. Only reindeer with his own hot tub.

✳ RUDOLPH — Sure, he may have been a misfit once, but from the first night Santa decided to let Rudolph's glowing nose guide the sleigh, he has been an unrepentant prima donna. Rudolph has not forgotten that all of the other reindeer used to laugh and call him names. He barely talks to his co-workers, and demands that his trough be filled with Evian. His relationship with Santa is equally strained; once having attained the leadership position, Rudolph has proved reluctant to relinquish it. As a result, Santa privately regrets that one foggy Christmas eve that started it all.

29. REINDEER GAMES

For thousands of years, the existence of reindeer games was unknown to the general populace, as these activities were considered a subset of the confidential operations of Claus Manufacturing, LLC. It was a former employee, in violation of the confidentiality agreement, who caused this information to be disseminated, resulting in the children's book and then the popular song that informed the world about Rudolph's origins.

(NOTE: The cog responsible for leaking this information has been relegated to a mall in Pawtucket, Rhode Island, where he is reduced to wrangling sticky children and handing them off to a drunken, belligerent, and largely incoherent department store Santa Claus. This fate is a common one among disloyal Claus Manufacturing, LLC, employees.)

Pawtucket? I dream of being in Pawtucket!

In order that cogs may have some idea of what they are witnessing as they make their way past the holding pens, here is a description of some of the more enduring games engaged in by Santa's reindeer:

Bite the Tick – A competitive game that grew out of the reindeer's enjoyment of shared grooming responsibilities. Two animals lunge at each other repeatedly, seeing how many ticks they can bite out of their opponent's fur in 60 seconds. A remarkable example of socialized behavior in the animal kingdom, it also generates quite a lot of office pools.

Antler Ball – Like soccer, if the entire game consisted of headers. An irregular plush toy from the Stuffed Animal Workshop serves as the ball. This game is very popular in Europe. Has not caught on in America yet.

Charades – Inexplicably popular among the eight pre-Rudolph reindeer. (Rudolph, fueled by his old resentments, refuses to play games with them anyway.) The classic party game is severely limited by the fact that reindeer have no fingers and can only hold up one hoof at a time. Therefore, play is confined to one-syllable words, which makes for very quick and not very challenging rounds. Still, the reindeer enjoy the game, and have gotten very skilled at interpreting each other's pantomimes, most of which look from afar like a quadruped version of Blue Man Group.

Wheel of Fortune – This is often frustrating to witness, owing to Dasher's tendency to buy a vowel even when she already knows what the answer is.

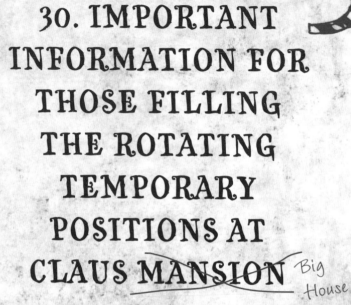

30. IMPORTANT INFORMATION FOR THOSE FILLING THE ROTATING TEMPORARY POSITIONS AT CLAUS ~~MANSION~~ Big House

All cogs rotate duties at the exclusive residence of our Chief Executive Officer and his wife. It is important for you not to think of "pulling estate time" (as some of your now-former employees once playfully called responsibilities at the mansion) as either a painful obligation or some kind of respite from your normal cog responsibilities in the workshop and its environs. Being given a daily or weekly assignment within the walls of Santa's stately pleasure dome is both a privilege and a grave responsibility. In this section you will find a helpful primer on what is expected of you at the residence of residences.

Keyword here is "grave."

Santa, like all great men, has many eccentricities. Long-term cogs have come to find them endearing, and we suggest that new hires also decide to find them so, and as quickly as possible. The owner of the largest still-active mythological retail operation in the free world did not get where he is by behaving just like everybody else. No, he got there by quickly establishing a power dynamic, and surrounding himself with underlings who have no vested interest in questioning how he does things. In this way, Santa assured that as his fame grew, he could develop many offbeat ways of coping with the pressures of his legend, and that these bizarre and often anti-social tendencies would be not only tolerated but completely unquestioned by his subordinates. We often tell new cogs at Claus Manufacturing, LLC, that their time at Claus Mansion calls for them to be part elf/part celebrity assistant.

translation: He's crackers!

part butt-kisser

Finally, information on the private life of Santa Claus is among the things most coveted by the unscrupulous of the world (all of whom have been getting nothing but coal in their stocking for quite a long time now, thank you very much). The less the general public knows about Santa, the more enigmatically and powerfully he will continue to loom in their imaginations. Really, it's pretty much Psych 101. In any case, do not jeopardize the very foundation of our corporate identity and its long-term financial return. At Claus Manufacturing, LLC, we've developed a simple little rhyming phrase to fall back on when it comes to working at the mansion:

When it comes to Saint Nick
You don't know Dick.

Responsibilities at Claus Mansion

Arrival in the Foyer — First and most important rule: wipe your feet! You can well imagine that after countless centuries of having to deal with snow during his rather intense commute on December 24, Santa is in no mood to have the stuff tracked all over his entryway. During the stress of peak production, Santa is actually able to spot 1/10 centimeter of snow on the floor before it even melts. Should he spot that infinitesimal amount on you, you will be made to go back outside into the snow, wipe your feet on the doormat once again, and re-enter the foyer with your boots snow- and moisture-free. Should any particle of snow escape your footwear and find its way to the floor again, the process will be repeated. Some new employees have been known to clock an entire day before getting past the foyer.

Information Relay — Each morning over breakfast, the Clauses sit on opposite ends of an enormously long oak table, easily 30 feet apart. Santa scans the *North Pole Intelligencer* for the day's stock quotes, while Mrs. Claus watches *Good Morning, Arctic Circle* on the television. Rarely will they have anything to say to one another, but if they should, an elf needs to be on hand to relay the information by dashing from one end of the table to the other. A typical exchange might go something like this:

SANTA
Tell her she squeezed the toothpaste tube
in the middle again this morning.

YOU
(*crossing to other end of table*) He said to tell you
that you squeezed the toothpaste tube
in the middle again this morning.

MRS. CLAUS
Tell him I'll squeeze the toothpaste however
I want to squeeze the toothpaste.

YOU

(crossing to opposite end of table) She said to
tell you that she'll squeeze the toothpaste
however she wants to squeeze the toothpaste.

SANTA

Well, you tell her that she knows it upsets me when
she squeezes the toothpaste tube in the middle,
and I am asking her nicely to knock it off.

YOU

(crossing to other end of table again) He said
to tell you that you know it upsets him when
you squeeze the toothpaste tube in the middle,
and he's asking you nicely to knock it off.

MRS. CLAUS

Is that so? Well you can tell Fat Boy that I'll
squeeze more than his toothpaste, and I mean
hard enough to do some damage!

And so on.

Coatroom Attendant — The fact that our CEO maintains a
wardrobe of 1,249 identical Santa Claus suits may be related

to either his anxiety/panic disorder or his obsessive-compulsive disorder. The sheer number of exactly-alike red and white coat/pant sets would seem to point to OCD; however, Santa's inexplicable need to suddenly swap the outfit he is currently wearing for a fresh one (from, incidentally, the largest walk-in closet since the reign of Mithridates II of Parthia) can occur as many as 50 times daily, which just may indicate a touch of anxiety.

Whatever the reason, it has become necessary to keep a Claus Manufacturing, LLC, cog nearby, to make sure newly brushed and lint-free Santa suits are ready whenever they are requested. Perhaps Santa has just had a run-in with Rudolph; perhaps the parent company has been breathing down his neck, demanding greater productivity; perhaps he has simply wassailed to excess ... one can never know for sure. What is evident is that our leader is flipping out, and the only way he can think to quell his inner confusion and imminent psychotic break is to put on a new Santa suit. A symbolic fresh start, the donning of the new uniform never fails to calm his spasmodic breathing and slowly bring his disposition back to normal. For at least 20 minutes.

Be warned: this job is not for the squeamish. Often Santa is so on top of his nerves that he has stripped naked by the time he arrives at the second-floor landing where the coatroom is located. Many an overzealous employee has been traumatized by the sight of a 350-pound nude man with an unruly grey beard demanding a change of clothing. DO NOT sign up for this duty unless you are absolutely certain you can remain the same after seeing the CEO's dangly bits. And if you are certain you can withstand such imagery, be prepared to be taken aside by an embittered Mrs. Claus, who will more than likely make a sardonic remark, usually along the lines of asking you what they look like since she has not seem them in quite some time.

Sparring Partner — One of the prides of Claus Mansion is the regulation boxing ring Santa had built in the east wing over 100 years ago. An amateur pugilist before taking up worldwide overnight gift delivery, Santa still uses the "sweet science" to unwind and cope with the demands of his job. And that's where you come in. Take a break from the assembly line, pull on a pair of gloves and some protective headgear, and let Santa try for the knockdown! (Look out, he's got a mean left jab, and throws a heck of a combination.)

NOTE: Intending no disrespect to our full-size human employees, Santa has mandated that it's just more fun for all concerned if this position is filled by elves only. He says that folks half his size are more agile and thus more evenly matched with him. This allows him to get the full benefit of unleashing all the week's pent-up aggression on someone more worthy of his experience: an elf. *As someone who filled this duty many times, may I just say . . . wait a minute, I forgot my name again . . . Um . . . uh . . . ADRIAN!!*

Wine Cellar Upkeep — Santa prides himself on his collection of fine wines, and each bottle must be thoroughly dusted every day. Many of the wines were given as gifts from the world's potentates in thanks for Santa's speedy delivery of toys to their offspring. On any given day, you may be dusting off the bottle of Chateau Latour sent in gratitude by Louis XIV, after Santa doubled back to France from the Ottoman Empire in just under 20 minutes to deliver a rocking horse; or the incredibly rare 15th-century red wine from Italy's Sangiovese region, given to Santa by Leonardo da Vinci's parents after Santa impulsively delivered a sketch pad to Leonardo instead of the yo-yo he had planned on originally; or the bottle of Port that Richard Nixon passed onto Santa in gratitude for finally being taken off the "naughty" list. Needless to say, you would be ill-advised to drop any of these one-of-a-kind wines. The last time one of his prize wines was destroyed, Santa sank into an ineffectual funk so deep that half the population of Liechtenstein didn't get their presents until Groundhog Day.

NOTE: Do not be alarmed if you find Mrs. Claus off alone in one corner of the wine cellar, swigging from a bottle of Merlot and talking to herself. You are not to approach her, or ask her if she needs anything, no matter how long and hard she is wailing or bemoaning her fate. This is simply her way of coping with the pressures of living with a great man. Luckily for our legal department, any phrases a cog may inadvertently overhear, such as "unrepentant womanizer," "incapable of intimacy" and "should have signed that pre-nup," are barely intelligible when slurred.

Guarding "Rosebud" — Santa's first boyhood sleigh is kept in its own fireproof safe in the rare arts storage room. You will be part of an around-the-clock, 24-hour rotating guard keeping watch on this valuable, centuries-old artifact. Certainly the childhood sleigh of Santa Claus would likely fetch millions on eBay, but according to Santa the guards are posted by Rosebud so that he may be assured that his memories are secure. There is a reason for this seeming mania about a small item kept in a locked safe with 28-inch-thick reinforced steel walls, and that reason is at the very heart of the man we are proud to call our boss, the CEO of Claus Manufacturing.

Get a life!

And now, as your final introduction to the inner workings of Claus Mansion, we would like to give you a little insight into the big, chortling man who resides there. We are proud to present a copyrighted feature of the North Pole Employee Handbook called:

Get to Know Your CEO (A Biography)

The year was 1287. As a child, the young Phil Claus ("Phil" was his given name—"Santa" came later as his reputation grew) was carefree, romping in the snowy Finnish countryside and learning about what an umlaut was. One Christmas, on a whim, he delivered presents to his three best friends (Järvinen, Venäläinen, and Harmaajärvi) using his diminutive sleigh, which he named "Rosebud" after his parents, Rose and Bud Claus.

Before long, Phil Claus's gift-delivery service became a local tradition in the village of Ruotsinpyhtää, and word began to spread to outlying areas that the young Claus had perhaps found his calling. At the same time, Rose and Bud Claus, simple reindeer herders, were approached by a wealthy industrialist who offered to buy eight of their prize animals (Donder et al).

The sale of the eight reindeer would at last relieve the Clauses of their mountain of debt, so they agreed, little knowing that the industrialist (his umlauted name is lost to history) had also heard tales of the 8-year old Phil Claus and his reputation for making Christmas special to the Ruotsinpyhtääians.

The wealthy man had visions of a bigger sleigh for Phil Claus, one pulled by eight flying reindeer, and one that would alter the course of world history. He convinced Rose and Bud to let him serve as Phil's guardian, raising the boy up in a new industry that would one day end the entire family's financial woes. It did, of course, but Phil was never able to return home before his parents passed away, and he was 50 before he realized that neither he nor his reindeer were aging. By then the "industrialist" had disappeared, though many say it was his guiding hand that arranged for the newly dubbed "Santa" Claus to meet his bride-to-be, Mildred, at a Helsinki lederhosen convention. Fifty years into their marriage, she, too, had not aged, and Santa's growing business needed a place in which to expand. The North Pole proved the perfect choice, its snowy environs reminding Santa and Mildred of their child-hood home (and its confusing jurisdictional authority just right for a non-union shop).

Who was the mysterious man who brought Santa Claus to his higher calling? We will never know. But what every Claus Manufacturing, LLC, cog must understand is that their boss is a man who paid a price for that calling. He was deprived of a normal childhood, taken away from the family he loved and given immense responsibility in tandem with immortality. It is no wonder he took to eating rich food as a balm for his troubled soul, washing it down with the tonic of laughter. In so doing, he truly became the jolly fat man whose visits are so treasured across the planet. And being immortal means he will never have to worry about his cholesterol. So, if you ever run into a human child, tell them to keep the cookies and milk coming.

Somehow little "Rosebud," the sleigh that represents a happier, simpler time in the life of the former Phil Claus, stayed with Santa throughout his long and storied journey. Often he will simply come to the rare arts room, pull out a folding chair, and sit by the safe in which the beginner sleigh is stored. In his more contemplative moments, Santa will talk quietly to whoever is on guard duty, allowing that fortunate cog to see a deeper, more soulful side to The Man. He may speak wistfully of the early days, before the world was so densely populated and he could complete his deliveries ahead of schedule, stopping off for a beer and a bump at Mongol's of Moscow; he may tell of the day Rudolph, the ninth reindeer, was unloaded on him by a traveling unguent salesman; or he may simply weep softly while humming "I'll Be Home For Christmas." Your job in these moments is to remain still and listen attentively. While you might be tempted to reach out and put a hand on Santa's shoulder, this is strongly discouraged.

And finally, whatever you do, don't call him "Phil."

31. ACTIVITIES AND COMMITTEES

We strongly encourage you to join up for one or more of our fun and diversionary activities or committees. We at Claus Manufacturing, LLC, feel that the last thing you need is to spend your down time in the troubled and questioning regions of your own mind. So if your position in the company has you finding yourself saying "Why are we here?" or "Oh, what's the point?" or "Life is simply an organism designed to feed the great sucking hole that is existence as we know it," why not sign up for the group activity of your choice today?

I tried a diversionary activity — look where it got me.

How about pin the tail on the fat jackass in a red suit?

There's so much to choose from!

a. The Greenland-Adjacent Gay Apparels — Our very own hockey team is feared throughout the 90° North Latitude region. Their take-no-prisoners attitude has led to 17 regional championships, and they have twice taken home the coveted Ice Cream Cup.

woo-hoo! Go Gay A's!

The Gay Apparels' regular season includes matchups with the walrus blubber industry's Fighting Foreflippers, the North Pole Uphill Battlers (made up of members from the North Pole Tourism Industry), and the always-formidable Bands of High Pressure, a team of local meteorologists.

There was a time when our high-stickers from Claus Manufacturing, LLC, would have to endure taunts from the opposing team (such as "Are your panty hose chafing?" or "Nice hat!"), but as the G.A.'s have long-since proven, hell hath no fury like an elf scorned.

Given our positive, nose-to-the-grindstone work environment, we're at a loss as to why the elves that sign up for our hockey team have so much aggression to vent. But don't you enlist in the G.A.'s unless you have tension from the working day that you want to take out on someone other than your employer!

And as long as our championship team is breaking the noses of those who stand in the way of victory, we won't stand in *their* way.

b. Elf Socials — Want to know about the background, likes, and dislikes of that elf you see across the assembly line each day, but never talk to because you're honoring unspoken company policy about unnecessary chatter during peak production? *no*

Feel like you may have opinions to share with your fellow elves, and often wonder what it might be like to engage in lively debate about vital issues of the day? *No*

Or do you just want to gorge on Christmas-stocking-shaped cookies, overindulge in egg nog, and cut a rug with another elf who shares your interests? *God no*

You can do all of these things at an Elf Social! *Damn*

It's a great way to unwind, and establish meaningful connections with your fellow cogs. *and other oxymorons*
Non-elves welcome! (Admission is only $10.00!)

And if I find out which one of those "fellow cogs" ratted me out. . .

NOTE: It is up to the individual cog to reconcile the highly interactive nature of the Elf Social with our strict anti-inter-employee dating policies. The encouraging of activities such as stimulating conversation, dancing, and the consumption of egg nog should in no way be construed as advocating anything of an icky nature.

Elf Socials: Banned Music

The following songs are banned from play during the dance portions of an Elf Social:

Song	Banned By	Reason
"Good King Wenceslas"	Santa	Knew Mr. Wenceslas, found him insufferably pious
Alvin & The Chipmunks, "Christmas Song"	Bowl Full of Jelly, Inc.	Chipmunk voices offensive to elves

The Nutcracker Suite	Santa	Never bought the whole toys-coming-to-life premise
"Do They Know It's Christmas?"	Bowl Full of Jelly, Inc.	Bono
"I Saw Mommy Kissing Santa Claus"	Mrs. Claus	Too close to home
Paul McCartney, *"Wonderful Christmastime"*	Santa, Mrs. Claus, Bowl Full of Jelly, Inc.	Makes ears bleed
"Frosty the Snowman"	Santa	Minor mythological figure hardly deserving of own song

"Blue Christmas"	Bowl Full of Jelly, Inc.	Depressing
"Santa Baby"	Mrs. Claus	Way too close to home
"YMCA"	Santa	Drives Dancer and (particularly) Prancer insane
Pink Floyd, "Another Brick in the Wall"	Bowl Full of Jelly, Inc.	No organization is ever aided by a timeless message of nonconformity

c. Yuletide Yoga — Santa first discovered yoga while delivering a toy elephant to the son of Akbar the Great in 1556. Ever since, he has encouraged the formation of an extra-curricular committee that offers its teachings to our cogs. Come in, pick a chakra, find your prana, chant a mantra, and tap into the ancient energy-restoring powers of this deeply spiritual practice. Then get back onto the assembly line and serve the forces of market-driven capitalism from a place of renewal and maximum efficiency. (Lab fee of $50 includes yoga mat, aromatherapy candle, and CD of wind chimes.)

d. Movie Night — For years, a lonely and melancholy Santa would sit alone in the private screening room at Claus Mansion, watching 16mm prints of classic films on a rickety old projector that cast a flickering glow on his sad, bearded countenance. With the advent of the VCR, Mrs. Claus encouraged him to invite the staff in for an old-fashioned evening at the pictures, and it proved just the tonic our CEO needed. And at just $4.00 a ticket, with popcorn and beverages in the affordable price range of $1.50–$3.75, this is one night out that won't break the bank!

So come on in through the special side entrance*, have a seat in our state-of-the-art mini-theater, and enjoy the magic of the movies!

*No access to rest of mansion once inside screening room

Movie Night: Banned Movies

The following films have been banned from public screening at Claus Manufacturing, LLC, Movie Nights:

Film	Banned By	Reason
Miracle on 34th Street	Santa	Department-store Santas are all dysfunctional drunks and should not have their delusions encouraged
A Christmas Story	Santa	Delightful until the department-store Santa kicks Ralphie down the slide (see above)
The Santa Clause	Santa	Atrocious play on words. Plus, Tim

[handwritten note: ONLY dept. store fatsos?]

		Allen wears a fat suit. (Did not even have the decency to gain weight for a role like DeNiro in *Raging Bull*)
It's a Wonderful Life	Bowl Full of Jelly, Inc.	George Bailey does not understand the fundamentals of a free market economy
Home Alone	Mrs. Claus	That annoying little boy
A Christmas Carol	Santa, Mrs. Claus, Bowl Full of Jelly, Inc.	Ebenezer Scrooge had a firm grasp on the fundamentals of a free market economy, and then blew it

National Lampoon's Christmas Vacation	Santa	Uninspired commentary track
Apocalypse Now, Natural Born Killers, the *Saw* films	Santa, Mrs. Claus, Bowl Full of Jelly, Inc.	Easily the least Christmas-y movies ever made.

How about —
Norma Rae
On the Waterfront
Hoffa

e. Weekly Newsletter Volunteer Committee — *The Poinsettia Press,* a three-page gatefold broadsheet, is the weekly photocopied voice of Claus Manufacturing, LLC, and we always need motivated volunteers to report on the issues that matter to the cog community. Work the city beat, write a column, compile the classifieds — this is your chance for a shot at journalistic glory! Here are just some of the long-running features that grace the pages of the *PP* every week:

North Pole Confidential — A scathing, no-holds-barred look into the inner workings of the North Pole and its mean streets. Recent exposés have featured such headlines as *Ice Remains Really Cold, People Are Freezing These Days,* and *Public Demands Stop Sign At Corner of 90° North and 0° West.*

Dear Flingle — Flingle the Elf (in reality any number of free-lance volunteers) has been answering Claus Manufacturing, LLC, cogs' delicate personal questions for decades in the *PP.* Readers have taken comfort in reading Flingle's recent stories *Depending on Where Mistletoe Is Hanging, Kissing Not Always Required; She Thinks He's Getting Some Wassailing on the Side;* and *Nosy Mother-In-Law Really Roasts His Chestnuts On An Open Fire.*

Claus Manufacturing, LLC, Business Report — A weekly appraisal of all the behind-the-scenes workings at Claus Manufacturing, LLC, known for its candid and unflinching coverage. Past stories such as *Claus Manufacturing, LLC, Doing Great; All Fears at Claus Manufacturing, LLC, Completely Unwarranted;* and *Things Have Never Been Better at Claus Manufacturing, LLC,* show that we're not afraid to tell it like it is.

It's your *PP.* Be part of it.

f. Book Group — Mrs. Claus has been leading the local ladies' book group for many years now, and it has proven to be one of the most popular after-work activities in the entire company. When the book group began, Mrs. Claus hosted the event in her study in Claus Mansion. As its popularity grew, Mrs. Claus soon saw how her husband became distracted and agitated at having so many elfin women in tights on the property, and a change in venue soon followed. It is now held in the laundry room at the employee housing cottage complex (the warmest room around!).

Hot mulled apple cider, intellectual companionship and lively discussion await the ladies who elect to take part in Mrs. Claus's Book Group. (P.S.: Non-ladies welcome!)

More than perhaps any other form of media, a book allows its reader to take in new, challenging and sometimes controversial ideas while broadening the mind and sharpening critical thinking skills. With this in mind, and per our parent company Bowl Full of Jelly, Inc., Book Group members should take note of some titles considered unsuitable for discussion in a public forum:

Book Group: Banned Books

Banned books include: *The Scarlet Letter, The Poky Little Puppy, Dr. Jekyll and Mr. Hyde, Walden, Gulliver's Travels, Moby Dick, A Farewell to Arms, The Odyssey, The Cat in the Hat, Lady Chatterley's Lover, The Lord of the Rings, A Portrait of the Artist as a Young Man, Paradise Lost, Charlotte's Web, Great Expectations, Candide, The Last of the Mohicans, The Canterbury Tales, On the Origin of Species, Animal Farm, Wuthering Heights, Of Mice and Men, The Little Prince, Pride and Prejudice, The Brothers Karamazov, Les Misérables, The Da Vinci Code, The Iliad, Brave New World, Madame Bovary, Winnie the Pooh and the Blustery Day, Jane Eyre, Robinson Crusoe, Anna Karenina, Heart of Darkness, War and Peace, The World According to Garp, Little Women, Alice's Adventures in Wonderland, Silas Marner, The Sound and the Fury, The Adventures of Huckleberry Finn, The Catcher in the Rye, Catch-22, Stephen King's "IT," The Hardy Boys and the Mystery of the Chinese Junk, Nancy Drew and the Secret of the Old Clock, Harry Potter and the Philosopher's Stone, Harry Potter and the Chamber of Secrets, Harry Potter and the Prisoner of Azkaban, Harry Potter and the Goblet of Fire, Harry Potter and the Order of the Phoenix, Harry Potter and the Half-Blood Prince, Harry Potter and the Deathly Hallows, Valley of the Dolls* ... (For complete list of banned books, see the six-page handout distributed at your orientation meeting.)

NOTE: As of the publication of this edition of the North Pole Employee Handbook, the following titles have been approved for reading and discussion at the Mrs. Claus Book Group evening:

1. *Rachael Ray's 30-Minute Get Real Meals*
2. *The Seven Habits of Highly Effective People*
3. *The Firm*

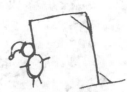

32. YOUR CAFETERIA

 s a Claus Manufacturing, LLC, cog, you will have to get used to being the envy of all your friends. After all, you work at a place where it's ~~Christmas~~ *HELL* all year 'round! And what better place to drive that point home than at your employee cafeteria?

Christmas is known for one thing: dessert! And that's a perfect fit for employees at Claus Manufacturing, LLC. Why? With 11.5 minutes for lunch, you want to get in, grab those energy-boosting sugars and starches and get back to the job. Best of all, our entire menu conforms to the standards of the well-known food pyramid, as required by the North Pole Department of Health.

Claus Cafeteria Menu

Breakfast—$8.95

Grains — Oatmeal Cookies
Milk & Dairy — Egg Nog
Vegetables — Pumpkin Pie
Fruit — Chef's own Figgy Pudding (We won't go until we get some!)
Meat — Mincemeat Pie (It's meat, but it's pie, too!)

Venison meat pie!

Lunch—$11.95

Grains — Yule log (with real bark)
Milk & Dairy — Rum & lactose-free milk (Try it!)
Vegetables — Squash Pie
Fruit — Fruitcake
Meat — Fruitcake (Last year's—could well be meat by now)

Dinner—$15.95

Grains — Pound Cake
Milk & Dairy — Cheesecake
Vegetables — Zucchini Cake
Fruit — Cranberry Cake
Meat — Pecan Cake (Meat group also includes nuts. We checked.)

Prix Fixe Menu includes dessert!

Unfortunately, we cannot offer employee discounts on cafeteria food. However, special consideration will be given to those willing to wash dishes.*

Executive Chef: Pepper Mintstix

*Time spent dishwashing does not count toward total hours worked.

33. HUNG BY THE CHIMNEY—YOUR COMPANY STORE

ince you'll be with us for at least the term of your three-year contract, it's good to know that thanks to our multi-purpose shopping centre, you'll have even fewer reasons to ever leave the North Pole!

From plungers to peanut butter, from bed sheets to bric-a-brac, from produce to printer ink, you're going to find everything you need for quality living right here at Hung By the Chimney.

IMPORTANT: SHOW YOUR EMPLOYEE ID FOR A 1.8% DISCOUNT ON ALL NON-FOOD ITEMS.

In addition to the basics, Hung By the Chimney features these fun-filled items, available exclusively to Claus Manufacturing, LLC, cogs:

"You Sleigh Me" Roof Landing Simulator — Think you have what it takes to do Santa's job? *Yes! That was the whole point!*

You'll find out when you slip on the headset goggles, grab the joystick, and try to navigate a reindeer-driven sleigh onto a variety of differently proportioned roofs representing 30 international dwellings. Settings include thatched hut, country cottage, Cape Cod, gated community, high-rise, tenement, and many others. Can you guide Rudolph and friends as you plummet from an airborne height of 36,000 feet to roughly 28 feet in just under nine seconds? Suddenly Santa's quite the bad ass, isn't he?

$59.95, or just $57.67 with your employee discount.

Jingle Bell Java™ — This is the coffee that keeps Santa humming! What did you think kept our man's energy going during the Christmas Eve delivery blitz? Sheer jocularity? Nope, it's the full-bodied smoothness of the boss's own signature java! And now you can take home a bag of your own joy juice ... wait until you see how much zing it puts in your swing shift! These beans have been grown especially for Santa in Brazil since1898, when that country's Princess Isabel sent several one-pound bags of the distinctive maragogype bean back with Santa in gratitude. (What she was thankful for remains a mystery, although Isabel's male descendents all have bushy white beards.)

$12.95/pound, or just $12.72/pound with your employee discount.

Tomas Cincaide, Elf Artist of Light*® *Garish Item Collection — A former cog turned internationally-renowned creator of taste-free art, Mr. Cincaide has been commissioned by Mrs. Claus as the exclusive artist of the North Pole. And we are pleased to offer Claus Manufacturing, LLC, cogs their 1.8% employee discount on any item in the Garish Item Collection. Choose from the Garish Little Village, the Garish Snowy Glade, the Garish Babbling Brook, the Garish Log Cabin, or the awe-inspiring three-dimensional sculpture, the Garish Carolers by the Tree. Only the finest art is battery operated!

$79.95–$750, or just $78.52–$736.50 with your employee discount.

The Gay Apparels — *150 Years of Not Giving a Puck* — This commemorative Blu-Ray disc of our very own hockey team features adrenaline-pumping highlights from several of their winning seasons. If you missed the game in which our 2-foot 4-inch forward Eric "Moonwisp" Springle hip-checked a 250-lb. defenseman from the Foreflippers into the cheap seats, you can see it here. If you've heard about our legendary (and colorful) late-19th-century goalie Jimmy the Jewelshaper Roth but never seen him in action, you'll delight in early kinescopes of his ice-bound hijinks. (Don't blink your eyes, or you won't see where he pulls that stick out of!) And, of course, no retrospective of the G.A.'s would be complete without plenty of coverage of our feisty elfin cheerleaders, the Big Girls!

$15, or just $14.73 with your employee discount.

34. SECRET SANTA

Our Secret Santa program really gives you a chance to show how much you care. Each employee buys a gift valued at or about $20 and gives it to Santa anonymously. That's right, you get to be Santa … for Santa!

Jeez, what an honor . . . NOT! Greedy S.O.B.!!!

Just ask some of the cogs who have served her the longest: of all the things company policy makes you spend money on while employed at Claus Manufacturing, LLC, the Secret Santa exchange is perhaps the most important one. It lets us know you're a team player. It demonstrates your understanding of Santa's emotional needs. And, in many non-verbal ways, it tells us that you want to keep something that has become very, very special to you: your job.

35. FAQ's

Q: *I'm a human, not an elf. Will I really be accepted here at Claus Manufacturing LLC?*
A: As long as you wear the ears.

Q: *Does Santa have any pet peeves?*
A: Beard pulling, rein burn, Microsoft Word.

Q: *What is the proper way to address Mrs. Claus?*
A: Her name is Mildred. You are welcome to try using it.

or try 'Fatso's Old Lady!' That works, too!

Q: *I'm a new employee, and I show up at the security gate one morning without my identification card. What can I do?*
A: When you are first hired, you will be asked to choose which celebrity you can do an (at least) passable impression of. If you arrive at the checkpoint having forgotten your ID, the security guard will have, next to your name on the

roster, the name of the celebrity whom you claim to be able to impersonate. Simply launch into your impersonation and, if it is indeed passable, you will be allowed through security. It's just another way we turn a negative (you forgot your ID) into a happy-go-lucky positive (you get to behave ridiculously in front of your fellow employees as they lose precious moments of their paid workday waiting for you to finish hamming it up). NOTE: If your impersonation is deemed less-than-convincing by security, you will be refused entry and be docked a day's pay. So brush up on that Jack Nicholson, chief!

Q: *Why am I asked to pay out of my own pocket for so many amenities and events at Claus Manufacturing, LLC?*
A: All fees charged to our cogs while they are under contract at Claus Manufacturing, LLC, go to a special fund. Every year, there is usually one human child somewhere who writes a letter to Santa in desperate need of a bone marrow transplant or with the fervent wish to meet their favorite sports hero before they die of a rare disease. Apparently, some of our employees think it unfair of the company to charge money for things. Such employees are just a little too selfish to want to see these beautiful, innocent children, already dealt such a cruel blow by fate,

miss out on the chance to become whole again. Are you wondering if there is any truth to this explanation? If you have to ask, then you already know the answer.

Q: *What does the "LLC" in "Claus Manufacturing, LLC" stand for?*
A: "Limited Liability Company." Remember that phrase, "limited liability." It is the cornerstone of our organization.

Q: *I have a problem and I want to take it up with my supervisor, but I haven't been told whom my immediate supervisor is. How can I find out?*
A: Let us answer your question with a question, cog. Are we not each of us our own supervisor? Are we not each responsible for the world we create? Does the wind move the sheet on the washing line, or is the sheet moving the wind? Or, to put it another way: if a complaint falls in the woods, and nobody is there to hear it, did it still challenge the status quo? These are questions with no answers. We hope this answers your question.

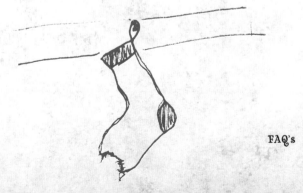

Q: *I entered the North Pole workforce as a Reindeer Droppings Engineer. What is my next lateral move* S.O.L.! *within the company?*
A: You will be able to advance into any position you desire as long as you have been properly disinfected.

Q: *Are there any ways I might not have thought of to help the operations at the North Pole go more smoothly?*
A: Stop sucking up to management, for one thing. (Kidding!)

Q: *What does "yule" mean?* Yule be sorry you were born an elf!
A: We have no idea.

Q: How can I stage a coup and let the people who do the REAL work run the show?

A: Forget it, PAL. The fat man has spies EVERYWHERE. You'll end up pissing your life away in Newark, New Jersey.

Supplemental Materials Exhibit I

CONFIDENTIALITY AGREEMENT
CLAUS MANUFACTURING, LLC

I, the undersigned, do hereby grant that, as an employee of Claus Manufacturing, LLC, I will, by virtue of necessity and proximity, come into contact with information as to the methods, policies, and technical operations of the company on a daily basis. About this I am to shut up.

Therefore I agree to hold all proprietary information (e.g., toy design, talking reindeer, the slowly devolving asexual relationship between Santa and Mrs. Claus) in strict confidence and not disclose such information to any third party.

I agree that any written communication I am given shall be subsequently destroyed by shredding, or, in the event of a power failure, eating.

I agree that at the conclusion of any discussions ("discussions" shall also include e-mails, PowerPoint presentations, jolly sing-alongs, and the like) regarding any aspect whatsoever of the daily operations of Claus Manufacturing, LLC, to submit to a voluntary brain wipe. (I acknowledge that, while not perfected, this is a harmless procedure that has no lasting effect on brain function. By still possessing the hand-eye coordination with which I am able to sign my own name to this document I am attesting to this finding.)

I agree to bite down on the pill located in the heel of my company-issued curly-toed shoe should any representative of a department store (e.g., Wal-Mart, Kmart, and, to a lesser extent, JC Penney) attempt to get anything out of me regarding how Claus Manufacturing, LLC, continues to remain profitable.

I agree to hold Santa Claus; Mrs. Claus; Claus Manufacturing, LLC; and Bowl Full of Jelly, Inc., blameless should the above occur. Granted, I will be dead in those circumstances, but perhaps surviving members of my family could prove meddlesome should I not agree to this part.

This agreement and its validity shall be governed by the laws of the North Pole.

AGREED AND ACCEPTED BY:

_____

(Cog)

_____

Date

FOR CLAUS MANUFACTURING, LLC

_____

S. Claus, CEO

_____

Milton R. Snowman
Snowman, Snowman, Snowman and Klein

Supplemental Materials Exhibit II

CLAUS MANUFACTURING, LLC
SAMPLE EMPLOYEE EVALUATION FORM

Date: _____

Cog: _____*Snarky*_____

Job Title: ___*In Jeopardy*_____

Interviewed by: Mrs. Claus [sample] *sample Mrs. Claus?*
_____ *I don't think so!*

RATINGS GUIDE:

5 - Superlative: Cog's performance is above expectations.

4 - Commendable: Cog's performance falls short of outstanding; cog recognizes need for improvement.

3 - So-So: Cog barely meets performance requirements, is ignorant of his/her unacceptable and very nearly foul nature.

2 - Pushing It: Cog is clearly flipping the organization the bird.

1 - Hideous: Cog is personally and professionally repugnant.

PERFORMANCE FACTORS:

1. Did cog arrive on time for this evaluation? _____
_____ If by "on time" you mean completely hammered.
RATING: 5

2. Is cog properly communicative? _Yes. I particularly liked_
his choice of parting words, "Blow it out your yule log!"
RATING: 5

3. Has cog developed a rapport with his/her fellow cogs?
The other cogs seem delighted by his ability to belch the alphabet.
RATING: 16

4. Has cog exhibited dependability? _____ Yes. _____
_____ Especially when it comes to public urination._
RATING: 4

5. Does cog have a good attitude? _He frequently speaks of_
ending it all to escape the mind-numbing pain of working here.
_____ I think that's a "yes."_
RATING: 1

6. Is cog thorough in his/her work? _Yes. Last week on the assembly line, he took the time to painstakingly carve the words "Please God help me" into the bottom of a child's toy, along with his contact information._

RATING: 5

7. Does cog have clear and established goals, and is he/she taking appropriate steps to achieve those goals? _He was until somebody ratted him out. I'm guessing it was Skanky — that suck-up!_

RATING: 11

8. Is cog making the proper use of his/her own special capabilities? _Yes. Snarky is truly gifted at contemplating the bile-inducing nature of his life at Claus Manufacturing, LLC, and excels at the kind of deep regret and self-hatred that would make some therapist very wealthy, except this dump doesn't cover mental health visits, so he may very well die of ennui, and then it will be on your head._

RATING: 5

9. What would cog count among his/her most notable on-the-job achievements in the past 30 days? _Getting this close to running the show_

RATING: 25

10. What would cog say are areas of his/her job performance
that could use improvement? _After many years of effort,_
still unable to touch nose with tongue.

RATING: 1

OVERALL SCORE _983_

RECOMMENDATION _Should be locked in room and_
made to listen to Mannheim Steamroller Christmas
Album continuously until all cognitive function is lost.

Supplemental Materials Exhibit III

CLAUS MANUFACTURING, LLC
GRIEVANCE FORM

Cog name _____

Date _____

Wronged By (choose one):
☐ Santa
☐ Mrs. Claus
☐ Rudolph

Nature of grievance (choose one):
☐ Falsely accused of wrongdoing
(Santa, Mrs. Claus exempt from this category)
☐ Improperly disciplined
(Santa, Mrs. Claus exempt from this category)
☐ Treated unfairly by Rudolph

Please briefly explain the circumstances of how you were wronged by Rudolph: _____

_____

_____

_____

Would you like to see any disciplinary action taken against Rudolph? _____

_____

_____

_____

What would you say is a suitable punishment for Rudolph?

_____

_____

_____

_____

Thank you for taking the time to communicate with us regarding your grievance.

Bowl Full of Jelly, Inc.

Supplemental Materials, Exhibit IV

CLAUS MANUFACTURING, LLC
INTERNAL FEEDBACK FORM

Cog name (not required) _definitely not Snarky_

Thank you for taking the time to express your viewpoint to your employers at Claus Manufacturing, LLC. _Least I could do, scumbags._

We value your opinion and want you to feel as if you play a vital role in the decisions that are made about your employment here. _I believe that's what they told Luca Brazzi._

What area of our operations do you feel could use improvement? _____
_____ Fewer morons!_ _____

_____ _____

What is the specific nature of your feedback regarding this aspect of Claus Manufacturing, LLC? _____
What part of "fewer morons" did you not understand?

_____ _____

Do you have evidence supporting your contention? _____

_____

_____ *The fact that Santa is a moron.* _____

In your opinion, do other cogs share your opinion about this
subject? _____ *What are you, completely clueless? Of course!* _____

_____

_____

Which other cogs are they, specifically? _____ *Oh. Now I get it.* _____

_____ *Later!* _____

_____

Thank you. We will be in touch.

Respectfully,
Team Claus

Supplemental Materials Exhibit V

RESPONDING TO LETTERS TO SANTA
WORKSHEET

Following are three examples of actual letters to Santa received here at the North Pole. Below each is a blank space in which to write what you think would be an appropriate response to that letter.

Return the completed worksheet, with your answers, to Mrs. Claus in Human Resources. She will provide you with input as to how to improve your letter-answering skills based on your responses to these sample letters. Each letter includes a few ideas to think about as you craft your response.

Tips:

❄ Remember that a child may not always get the toy he or she requests, and to stress that Santa is busy and will do his best to get the child exactly what he or she wants. Emphasis should be put on how terrific it will be to get a gift direct from Santa, so that if it is not the requested gift, the child will still feel special.

❄ Try to think in Santa's voice. This does not mean you simply include "ho, ho, ho" in every sentence, but that you should imagine your boss, our CEO, smiling as he hands over a gift-wrapped present to a beaming child. This will put you in the proper warm-hearted place to respond properly.

❄ Avoid references to parents. You just never know what family unit your letter is going to anymore, and making a cheery remark about a child's "father," for example, may only remind them of an inveterate drunk who left home six years ago with his secretary and only visits on days that the court orders him to do so.

LETTER #1

Dear Santa,

I want a red bike for Christmas! That would be great.
And my sister wants a scooter.

Love,

Nathan, age 5

(Things to think about: Nathan's age and emotional
development; the color red; Nathan obviously likes his sister
enough to ask for something for her.)

Your response:

Dear Nathan,

How does it feel to want, ya little pissant?

Big hugs,

Santa

LETTER #2

Dear Santa,

What is it like at the North Pole? Do you get cold ever? Are you friends with your reindeer? Please say hi to Mrs. Claus for me. I would love to meet you someday.

If you can manage it, I would like a Barbie play set. Thank you, Santa!!!

Maureen, age 7

(Things to think about: Maureen asks a lot of questions about Santa's daily life; she is curious about the reindeer and Mrs. Claus; she saves her gift request for last.)

Your response:

Dear Maureen,

I don't really know what it's like at the North Pole, because I sit on my **LARD BUTT** all day ordering people around and that is my whole worthless life.

My reindeer are a bunch of codependent freaks that keep wanting to turn left when I know we should turn right. I hope you never meet me because it would shatter your illusions and very probably traumatize you for life, especially if you heard me curse, which I can do at the drop of a hat. And as for Barbie, how about you get smart and stop asking for toys that provide unrealistic expectations about what a woman is supposed to be?

Get lost,

Santa

LETTER #3

> Dear Santa,
>
> My mommy has appendix-itis, and my daddy needs
> a job. I don't want a toy this Christmas, only for
> everyone to be happy. Thank you, and I hope you
> have a great Christmas.
>
> Love,
>
> Ricky

(Things to think about: There are things more important
than toys; a child is looking for help; Ricky even takes the
time to wish Santa well.)

Your response:

Hey, Ricky!

I am sorry that things are bad at home right now. You will get over it a lot faster if you STOP writing to ineffectual losers like me and grow a backbone. As for everyone being HAPPY, somebody up here tried to make that happen. I SHIPPED HIS ASS OFF TO NEWARK! And you're not fooling anyone by wishing me a merry Christmas. You suck-ups are so transparent.

Get a life,
Santa

Supplemental Materials, Exhibit VI

WORK SONGS LYRIC SHEET

Remember that skill in *a cappella* singing is one of our five core competencies, and that you might be asked at any time to help motivate yourself and others through song. Here is a compendium of our most popular work songs for you to read, memorize, and utilize throughout your three-year contracted stay at Claus Manufacturing, LLC.

1. HERE COME BABY HEADS

Sung to the tune of "Here Comes Santa Claus"

Here come baby heads, here come baby heads
Down the assembly line
One, two, three, four, five, six, seven ... and baby heads
　　eight and nine!
Take one head and pass it on, be proud and stand up tall
'Cause at the North Pole "making babies" doesn't mean
　　what you think at all.

Here come baby heads, here come baby heads
Get one while they're hot
Attach it to a baby body and now look what you've got
A toy to bring great joy to children is made
　　when you are done
'Cause we can't have no headless babies frightening
　　everyone!

(REPEAT 50X)

2. WRAP THE PRESENTS

Sung to the tune of "Deck the Halls"

Wrap the presents very quickly
Fa-la-la-la-la, la-la-la-la
Stuff them into sacks quite briskly
Fa-la-la-la-la, la-la-la-la
Certainly you might be tired
Fa-la-la, la-la-la, la-la-la
Don't complain or you'll get fired
Fa-la-la-la-la, la-la-la-la

Load the sacks into the sleigh, now
Fa-la-la-la-la, la-la-la-la
Christmas will be any day now
Fa-la-la-la-la, la-la-la-la
So what if you have a conniption
Fa-la-la, la-la-la, la-la-la
This was in your job description
Fa-la-la-la-la, la-la-la-la

Santa's happy, you can bet it
Fa-la-la-la-la, la-la-la-la
Overtime, well we won't get it
Fa-la-la-la-la, la-la-la-la

Still, the world is getting gifted
Fa-la-la, la-la-la, la-la-la
All because we stooped and lifted
Fa-la-la-la-la, la-la-la-la!

(REPEAT 30X)

(REPEAT 200X on Christmas Eve)

3. PAY OF TWENTY GRAND

Sung to the tune of "Winter Wonderland"

Workbell rings, are you listenin'?
In the dawn, snow is glistenin'
We're up at the crack
We're one of the pack
Happy with our pay of twenty grand

Gone away is the light shift
Here to stay is the night shift
It's all in the cause
Of working for Claus
Happy with our pay of twenty grand

Every day the workshop is a buzzin'
With the blood and sweat that we provide
If you think that is a problem, cousin
It's nothing when your heart is filled with pride!

Later on, we're still workin'
But as long as coffee's perkin'
We're still good to go
We never are low
Happy with our pay of twenty grand

If we ever hear a colleague moanin'
We'll report him to the folks in charge
And the supervisor we'll be phonin'
To say there is a Gloomy Gus at large

It might be worth a mention
There's no room for dissention
We're here at the Pole
We're playing our role
Happy with our pay of twenty grand
Happy with our pay of twenty grand
Happy with our pay of twenty grand

(REPEAT UNTIL ORDERED TO STOP)

4. GOTTA SEW

Sung to the tune of "Let It Snow"

Oh, the stress of this job is frightful
But the product is so delightful
Stuffed animals are all we know
Gotta sew, gotta sew, gotta sew

Oh, it hardly shows signs of stopping
You can hear our wrist bones popping
But Teddy Bears run the show
Gotta sew, gotta sew, gotta sew

When we finally stitch one up
Seems another one takes its place
A plush little horse or pup
With a strange and expressionless face

Still, we never lose our perspective
That's the toy workshop directive
Where else are we gonna go?
Gotta sew, gotta sew, gotta sew

(REPEAT FOR AT LEAST 100 TEDDY BEARS)

5. COMPANY COG

Sung to the tune of "Jingle Bell Rock"

Company, company, company cog
That's what I am, dear sir or madam
I'm representing the corporate way
And I'm here to do what they say

Company, company, company cog
Towing the line, with me that is fine
Happy and striving to never be dull
I've read the manual!

If I am wise, I'll know I symbolize
The vision of the LLC
Therefore I vote not to rock the boat
Or bad mouth Santa on TV

I'm an e-ssential part of what we do
I'm like the "egg" in "nog"
More than a worker or employee or crew
That's the company
That's the company
I'm a company cog!

(REPEAT AS OFTEN AS NECESSARY)

No comment

About Cider Mill Press
Book Publishers

Good ideas ripen with time. From seed to harvest, Cider Mill Press strives to bring fine reading, information, and entertainment together between the covers of its creatively crafted books. Our Cider Mill bears fruit twice a year, publishing a new crop of titles each spring and fall.

*Where Good Books Are
Ready for Press*

Visit us on the Web at
www.cidermillpress.com
or write to us at
12 Port Farm Road
Kennebunkport, Maine 04046